Contents

Any words appearing in the text in bold, **like this**, are explained in the glossary.

What is a pond?

A pond is a small area of **fresh water**. The water in a pond is still. It does not flow like the water in a river or stream. A pond is much smaller than a **lake**.

Raintree

www.raintreepublishers.co.uk
Visit our website to find out more information about Raintree books.

To order:
☎ Phone 0845 6044371
🖹 Fax +44 (0) 1865 312263
🖳 Email myorders@raintreepublishers.co.uk

Customers from outside the UK please telephone +44 1865 312262

Raintree is an imprint of Capstone Global Library Limited, a company incorporated in England and Wales having its registered office at 7 Pilgrim Street, London, EC4V 6LB – Registered company number: 6695582

Text © Capstone Global Library Limited 2010
First published in hardback in 2010
Paperback edition first published in 2011
The moral rights of the proprietor have been asserted.

Edited by Charlotte Guillain, Nancy Dickmann, and Catherine Veitch
Designed by Joanna Hinton-Malivoire
Picture research by Elizabeth Alexander and Ruth Blair
Original illustrations © Capstone Global Library
Original illustrations by kja-artists (pp. 12-13, 29)
Original illustrations by Joanna Hinton-Malivoire (pp. 24, 28)
Production by Victoria Fitzgerald
Originated by Capstone Global Library Ltd
Printed and bound in China by Leo Paper Products

ISBN 978 0 431 17241 5 (hardback)
14 13 12 11 10
10 9 8 7 6 5 4 3 2 1

ISBN 978 0 431 17248 4 (paperback)
15 14 13 12 11
10 9 8 7 6 5 4 3 2 1

British Library Cataloguing in Publication Data
Ganeri, Anita.
Ponds. -- (Nature trails)
577.6'3-dc22

Acknowledgements
We would like to thank the following for permission to reproduce photographs: p. **20** © Capstone Global Library (Debbie Rowe); Corbis pp. **4-5** (© Adam Woolfitt), **7** (© Jon Sparks), **11** (© Image Source), **16** (© Hans Pfletschinger/Science Faction); iStockphoto pp. **14** (© Oleg Fedorkin), **18** (© Steve Byland), **22** (© Viorika Prikhodko), **25** (© Daniel Cooper), **27** (© Nina Matyszczak), **23 top** (© Andrew Howe); Photolibrary pp. **6** (© Robert Harding Travel), **8** (Geoff Higgins), **9** (© Garden Picture Library), **15** (Daniel Vega/age footstock), **21** (© Juniors Bildarchiv), **26** (© Panorama Stock RF); Shutterstock p. **23 bottom** (© wagtail).

Cover photograph of a frog in a garden pond in Clitheroe, Lancashire reproduced with permission of Corbis (© Ashley Cooper).

The publisher would like to thank Emma Shambrook for her assistance in the preparation of this book.

A pond is a type of **habitat**. A habitat is a place where plants and animals live. Many different plants and animals live in and around ponds in Britain.

In this book, the Signpost boxes ask you to find out more about animals and plants. Ask an adult to help you find information in books at school, in the library, or on the Internet.

Different ponds

There may be a pond in your garden or local park. These ponds were made for people to enjoy. Other ponds were dug in farmyards for animals to drink from.

Some ponds were not made by people. They formed in dips or hollows on **moorlands** or hills. The dips or hollows filled up with rainwater or melting snow to make ponds.

Changing ponds

If you watch a pond throughout the year, you will see lots of changes. In summer, ponds are full of life. Insects fly above the water. Fish, frogs, and toads feed on the insects.

Lots of insects are flying over this pond in summer.

Never walk on a frozen pond.
If the ice breaks you could fall in.

Winter is a difficult time for pond wildlife.
Sometimes, the water can freeze over.
Some plants and animals sink to the
bottom and hide in the mud. Other birds
and insects move away from the pond to
find shelter.

Exploring a pond

A good way to explore a pond is to go **pond dipping**. Scoop your net through the water and tip it into your bucket. Use your magnifying glass to look for small animals and plants. Handle pond plants and animals very gently, and put them back in the pond when you have finished looking at them.

What to take with you

- ✓ A fishing net
- ✓ A bucket or jar, filled with pond water
- ✓ A smaller, white plastic pot, filled with pond water, for looking at interesting finds
- ✓ A spoon for moving animals into the smaller container and back into the pond
- ✓ A magnifying glass
- ✓ A notebook and pencil

STAY SAFE

- Always take care near water and take an adult when you visit a pond.
- Do not get too close to the edge of the pond, or you could fall in.
- Wash your hands after pond dipping and cover up any cuts.

The best time to go pond dipping is in the spring and summer.

Pond plants

Different types of plants live in different parts of the pond. They have special **features** to help them live there. For example, rushes grow around the edges of a pond. They have strong **roots** to hold them firmly in the soft mud.

Canadian pondweed

spiked water milfoil

water–starwort

frogbit

deep water zone

The different zones of a pond

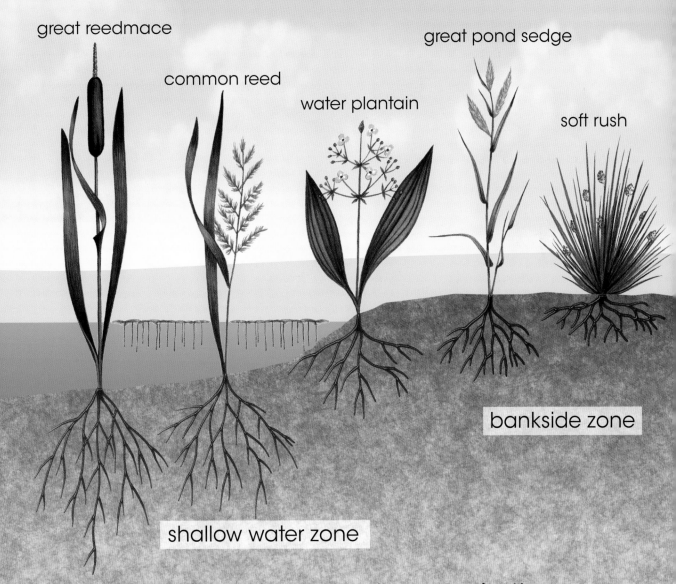

great reedmace

common reed

water plantain

great pond sedge

soft rush

bankside zone

shallow water zone

Some plants, such as reeds, grow in the **shallow** water at the edge of the pond. They are usually tall, with long, creeping roots to hold them upright.

13

More pond plants

waterlily

The leaves soak up sunlight that the plants need to make food.

Some plants float on the surface of the pond. Their roots grow in the mud on the bottom. Their leaves and stems are full of air that helps them float in the water.

Some plants live mostly under the water. They have long, fine leaves and stems which trail in the water so they do not get damaged. In summer, look for their flowers growing above the **surface**.

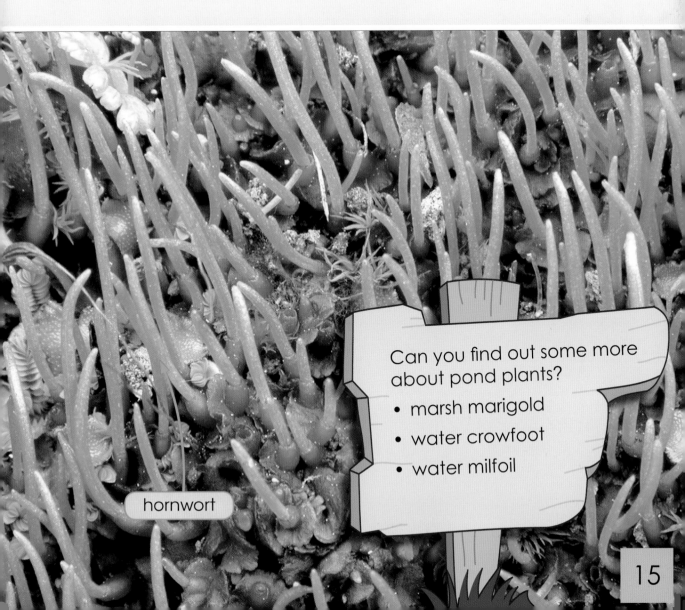

hornwort

Can you find out some more about pond plants?

- marsh marigold
- water crowfoot
- water milfoil

Pond minibeasts

Many insects and **minibeasts** live in and around ponds. Look in the air, on the water's surface, and in the water itself. These are all places where minibeasts hunt for their food.

A diving beetle dives underwater, carrying a bubble of air to breathe.

Count and record

Can you count some of the different kinds of insects in the pond? Spend fifteen minutes counting the insects you can see flying above the pond, floating on the surface, and swimming underwater. Record them in a **bar chart** like this one.

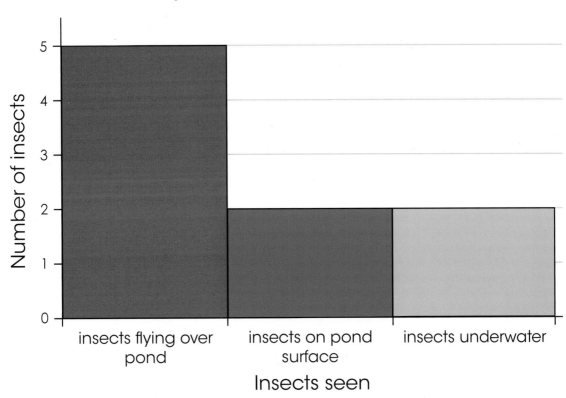

Bar chart showing the number of insects at a pond

Number of insects

5
4
3
2
1
0

insects flying over pond | insects on pond surface | insects underwater

Insects seen

Frogs and toads

Frogs and toads are animals, called **amphibians**. This means that they are born in water but spend most of their lives on land. They come back to the pond in spring to **breed**.

STAY SAFE

• Never hurt pond animals or pull up plants.
• If you catch something in your net, put it straight into your bucket. Use a spoon to put anything interesting in your white plastic pot. Then put it back into the pond as quickly as possible.

The life cycle of a frog

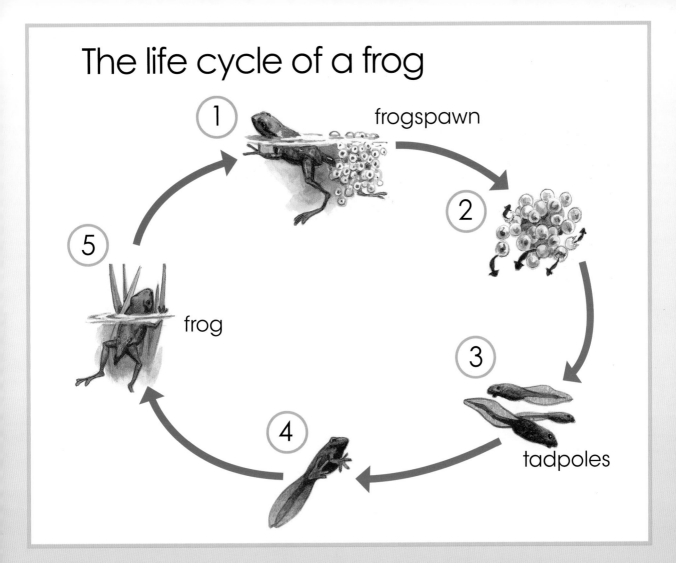

Female frogs lay hundreds of jelly-like eggs in the water. These eggs are called frogspawn. The eggs hatch into tadpoles that look and swim like tiny fish. As the tadpoles grow, their bodies change into little frogs.

Looking for fish

Pond fish are often rounder and fatter than fish that live in rivers and streams. They swim more slowly, too. They feed on plants, insects, worms, and other fish.

These goldfish have been put into a pond by people.

Fish can be hard to spot in ponds. Some hide in the plants around the pond edges. Others live too deep down to see. Stand quietly on the bank and look out for dark shapes swimming in the water.

perch

Can you find out some more about pond fish?

- pike
- stickleback
- minnow

Birds around the pond

Many birds live around ponds. Some live there all of the time. Others come to find food, drink, and have a bath. Some birds use ponds as places to build their nests.

A good place to watch birds is your local park pond. Look for ducks **dabbling** or diving for food. Can you spot any coots and moorhens? You can tell them apart by their beaks. Coots have white beaks. Moorhens have red beaks.

coot

moorhen

Can you find out some more about pond birds?

- kingfisher
- tufted duck
- grebe
- teal
- pintail

More pond birds

Some birds have special feet to help them live near ponds. Ducks, geese, and swans have **webbed** feet for swimming. Moorhens and coots have long, thin toes to stop them sinking into the soft mud.

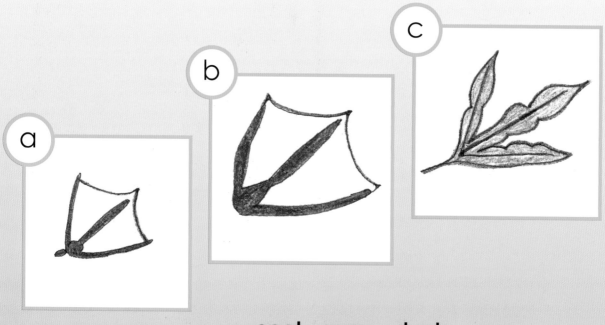

coot   swan   duck

Can you work out which birds made these **tracks**? Match each bird to a track. Ask an adult to help you find out the answer.

heron

A heron eats fish. It stands very still in the water, waiting for a fish to swim by. Then it stabs its long, sharp beak into the water and grabs the fish. It also catches frogs and tadpoles.

Ponds in danger

Many ponds are in danger. Some dry up over time. Others fill up with rubbish left by people. Rubbish makes ponds dirty and it also kills pond animals and plants.

This pond has dried up. Almost all of the water has gone.

You can help look after ponds by taking care when you visit them. Never leave any rubbish behind and clear up any litter you find lying around. Wear thick gloves to do this, and ask an adult for help.

More things to do

There are a lot more things you can do by a pond.

Making a pond plant map

Draw the shape of the pond in your notebook. Add any rocks or large trees. Then look at each section of the pond in turn and draw the plants you see on your map. You do not need to draw the plants in detail, just fill in blocks of colour.

A pond map

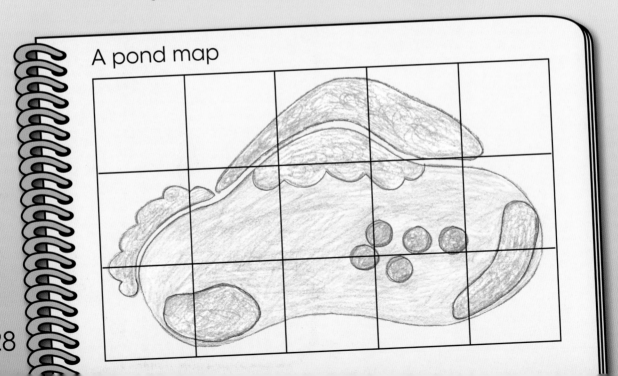

Looking at frogspawn

To see how tadpoles hatch out of eggs, collect a small amount of frogspawn in a jar of pond water. Take it home and put it into a larger container, like an **aquarium**, filled with more pond water and plants. Change the water twice a week. When the tadpoles hatch, take them back to the pond so they can grow into frogs.

Glossary

amphibians animals, such as frogs and toads, that live on water and on land

aquarium large tank for keeping fish and other water creatures in

bar chart diagram where numbers of things are shown by different coloured blocks

breed when animals have young

dabbling when ducks skim the surface of the water with their beaks for food

features special parts of a plant's or animal's body that helps it survive

fresh water water in ponds, lakes, and rivers, that is not salty

habitat place where animals and plants live

lake large area of fresh water

minibeasts small animals, such as spiders, snails, and worms

moorlands hilly land with boggy soil and plants, such as heather and moss

pond dipping using a net to catch and look at pond plants and animals

roots parts of a plant that grow down into the ground

shallow water that is not very deep

surface top layer of the water

track mark on the ground left by a person, animal, or thing

webbed feet that have skin stretched between the toes or claws

Find out more

Books to read

Eyewitness: Pond and River, Steve Parker
(Dorling Kindersley, 2003)

Look What I Found! By the Pond, G. Barker and
P. Humphreys (Franklin Watts, 2005)

Spotter's Guide to Ponds and Lakes
(Usborne Publishing, 2006)

Websites and organizations

Pond Conservation
www.pondconservation.org.uk
This national charity is dedicated to creating and
protecting ponds and the wildlife.

Young People's Trust for the Environment
www.ypte.org.uk
This charity aims to encourage young people's
understanding of the environment.

The Wildlife Trusts
www.wildlifetrusts.org
This is a voluntary organization dedicated to looking
after Britain's wildlife and habitats.

Index